Buddhism
How To Practice Buddhism In Your Everyday Life

Copyright © 2012 Elias Axmar
All rights reserved.

Contents

Introduction 5

Chapter 1: Buddhism-Detailed Insight Into Buddhism And How It Came Into Being 6
- How Did Buddhism Come into Being? 6
- Is Buddhism A Religion Or Not? 7

Chapter 2: Teachings Of Buddhism 9
- Way Of Investigation 9
- Four Noble Truths 9
- Eightfold Path 10
- Kamma 11
- Rebirth 11
- No Creator Or God 11
- Illusion Of Your Soul 11

Chapter 3: How You Can Benefit From Buddhism 13

Chapter 4: Fighting Stress, Anxiety And Depression With Buddhism 14
- Eliminate Stress And Depression With Meditation 14
- Mudras For Fighting Stress 15
- Starting Your Day With Positive Motivation And Thoughts 16

Chapter 5: Becoming Happier With Buddhism . 18
- Exercise Mindfulness To Become Aware Of Your Blessings 18

Chapter 6: Buddhism Practices For Improving Your Health And Sleep Related Problems 20
- Offering Food To Buddha 20
- Mindful Eating 20
- Mudras For Losing Weight, Improving Health, And Sleeping Better 20

Chapter 7: How To Improve Your Relationships

And Professional Life With Buddhism 23
Practice Right Livelihood 23
Become Mindful Of Your Relationships 23
Conclusion 25

Introduction

I want to thank you and commend you for opening the book, *"Buddhism: How to Practice Buddhism in Your Everyday Life"*.

This book contains actionable information on how to practice Buddhism in your daily life.

'Better than a thousand hollow words is one word that brings peace.'- Buddha

This beautiful, meaningful quote by Buddha, the founder of Buddhism sums up the basic essence of Buddhism. This book is going to help you better understand what Buddhism is, how it can benefit you, and how you can apply it in your routine life.

Some people refer to Buddhism as a religion, whereas many others call it a way of life and doing things the way they are. Whether it is a religion or not, it preaches peace and it provides you with guidelines that can help you live your life peacefully, happily and successfully. Buddhism provides you with deep information related to the worldly pleasures, your desires, and everything that prevents you from acquiring inner peace and happiness. Moreover, it also guides you on how you can battle all your obstructions, both the inner and outer ones, to gain complete peace of mind.

If you want to improve your understanding of Buddhism, you have landed at the right place. Continue reading this book to find out how Buddhism can be of help to you.

Thanks again for opening this book.

Chapter 1: Buddhism-Detailed Insight Into Buddhism And How It Came Into Being

Buddhism is a philosophy, some refer to it as a religion, or a faith, that comprises of numerous beliefs, spiritual practices and traditions based primarily on the teachings of Gautama Buddha. Let us dig deeper into this and find out more about Buddhism.

How Did Buddhism Come into Being?

Buddhism was founded by Siddharta Gautama Buddha, who is also known as 'Buddha', which means the awakened one. Sidharta Gautama was born around 2600 years back as a prince in a wealthy family that ruled a small area located near the current border shared by India and Nepal. He enjoyed all the luxuries of life and lived a lavish life. Despite all the comforts, Sidharta always felt a certain uneasiness and seldom found himself peaceful.

Sidharta often used to visit the capital of the kingdom. Mostly, he came across sick and old people living a life full of suffering. This left a strong impression on him and made him understand that everyone had to experience the pain and sufferings of being born, getting sick, getting old and then dying. Since he believed in reincarnation, he realized that these sufferings would not stop occurring. However, he was determined to find a solution for ending these sufferings and he knew he couldn't do this while living in the palace, so he decided to leave it.

When he was 29 years old, Sidharta left the palace and his family in search for the real meaning and purpose of life. He spent years in secluded forests, remote mountains, and villages of northeast India. He studied different religions and faiths under many wise philosophers and religious teachers. Nonetheless, he discovered whatever he learned did not satisfy him. He struggled alone for a long time, practicing asceticism and self-mortification, but all his efforts ended in vain.

He finally traveled to a town close to Bodh Gaya located in India. Over there, he started meditating and focused entirely on dharmakaya meditation. Dharmakaya corresponds to the enlightenment of the mind. Sidharta started training himself in the dharmakaya meditation and after six years; he started feeling content and believed that he was quite close to reaching complete enlightenment.

When he was 35 years old, he was sitting under a humungous tree on the night of the full moon of the 4th month corresponding to the 'lunar' calendar. That tree is now referred to as 'Boddhi tree.' He started meditating and promised himself that he wouldn't get up until he acquired complete enlightenment. He entered a space-like concentration corresponding to the dharmakaya. He continued with this practice until dawn and by that time, he had successfully attained full enlightenment, and had deciphered the true meaning, purpose and way of life. This enlightenment wasn't a type of revelation given by a divine being. Rather, it was a discovery that he made by meditating on the highest and deepest level and by acquiring a clear experience of the mind. By achieving enlightenment, Sidharta had cleansed himself of all the cravings, delusions, ill will, and desires and had founded the technique of living a harmonious life. From that time onwards, Sidharta was referred to as the Buddha, the enlightened one.

From this knowledge of how Buddhism came into being, is it a religion or not?

Is Buddhism A Religion Or Not?

Though the popular belief regarding Buddhism is that of a religion, in reality, it isn't a religion. Buddhism goes far beyond the concept of religion and is basically a way of living your life. Religion refers to a system of practices, behaviors, and views that are provided to you by a divine being. Whether it is Christianity, Judaism, Islam, or Hinduism- every religion is based on the existence of a supreme being that nurtures the world and everything it entails. On the other hand, Buddhism does not follow this concept.

Though Buddhism was started and developed by Gautama, Buddhists do not believe him to be a divine being nor do they seek refuge from him in the hope and faith that Buddha is going to save them. Buddhism is based on the mere concept of understanding and reasoning, known as 'samma-ditthi.' Buddha said,

"Do not accept anything on (mere) hearsay -- (i.e. thinking that thus have we heard it for a long time). Do not accept anything by mere tradition -- (i.e., thinking that it has thus been handed down through many generations). Do not accept anything on account of mere rumors -- (i.e. by believing what others say without any investigation). Do not accept anything just because it accords with your scriptures. Do not accept anything by mere suppositions. Do not accept anything by mere inference. Do not accept anything by merely considering the reasons. Do not accept anything merely because it agrees with your pre-conceived notions. Do not accept anything merely because it seems acceptable -- (i.e., thinking that as the speaker seems to be a good person his words should be accepted). Do not accept anything thinking that the ascetic is respected by us (therefore it is right to accept his word)."

Though Buddha did develop his own set of teaching, nonetheless, he didn't invite his followers, or other people to place blind faith in them.

He asked them to dig deeper into every idea and concept they come across to find out the truth behind it. This shows that Buddhism is a philosophy much broader than a religion and cannot be defined as a religion.

Chapter 2: Teachings Of Buddhism

Now that you have the basic idea of what Buddhism is, how it evolved and who Buddha was, let us find out what this philosophy teaches us. Having attained enlightenment, Buddha started teaching Dhamma, which means the true nature of everything. He travelled and taught the complete code of life for about 45 years. Even though, his teachings are quite deep, I will try to give you an overview of them, so you can get a basic understanding of what Buddhism teaches you.

Way Of Investigation

Buddha's very first teaching was to investigate everything and not accept anything based on blind faith. He advised people to inquire the truth of everything and anything that they came across. He pointed out that most of the problems were induced by believing on things based on tradition, hearsay and following an authority figure. The right way of accepting things is to have an open mind and dig deeper into the origin, development, and characteristics of things, so you know the truth about them. Similarly, he said that people should only accept his teaching after investigating them using meditation.

Four Noble Truths

During the course of his life, especially while striving to acquire enlightenment, Buddha discovered the four noble truths. These are the truths you need to accept and understand if you want to attain complete peace and happiness in life.

The first truth is the 'Truth of Dukkha', which states that each one of us is afflicted with some sort of suffering in this world. These sufferings are of two kinds: mental and physical. Mental afflictions are the emotional disturbances we experience after going through a hardship or difficult time in our life and physical suffering refers to the physical pain, injury, and harm we experience.

The second truth is 'the truth regarding the origin and creation of dukkha'. This truth states that the main cause of suffering is your ignorance and cravings. Ignorance is not being conscious of the reality of things and living a life of delusion. Craving refers to all your desires and wants that make you indulge in wrong practices that bring different kinds of harm and pain to you.

The third truth is 'the truth pertinent to the ending of all suffering'. This truth states that by working on eliminating all types of negativity and ill-centered things from your mind and life, you can get rid of all your sufferings and acquire the state of Nirvana, which is a state characterized by complete peace, happiness and serenity.

The fourth truth is 'the truth of following the middle way that ends all dukkha'. This truth states that to acquire nirvana, you need to follow the middle way, also known as the eightfold noble path. By following this path, you live a balanced life, which is neither too careless, nor too hard. It is just perfect and helps you live a beautiful life.

Eightfold Path

The eightfold noble path, or the middle way sets out the guidelines you need to follow to deal with all sorts of hardships and sufferings. This way of life comprises of eight rules that you need to follow:

- Samma Ditthi or Right View/ Understanding: You need to rectify your understanding of things and view things the right way to gain complete insight into them. This means correcting your view of this life and not getting attracted to the worldly pleasures because when this happens, you become engrossed in this world and strive to acquire those pleasures that result in suffering. Secondly, you need to understand that you inflict suffering on yourself, so to end it; you need to correct your vision.

- Samma Sankappa or Right Thought: Secondly, you need to focus on correcting your thought, which can be accomplished if you correct your intention. For that, you need to reject the worldly pleasures and bring kindness, love, and compassion for others in your thoughts.

- Samma Vacca or Right Speech: You need to work on correcting your speech, which can be done if you practice abstinence from slanderous speech, gossip, backbiting, cruel speech, and idle chitchatting.

- Samma Kammanta or Right Action: You must improve your actions and correct them by cleansing them from all sorts of sexual misconducts, illegal and destructive actions.

- Samma Ajiva or Right Livelihood: You need to correct your means of earning a living and must not do anything that harms any living being. Buddha instructed that you must not practice five professions: dealing in ammunition and arms, dealing in flesh (butcher), dealing in sex and human trafficking, dealing in any sort of drugs and dealing in any poisonous substance.

- Samma Vayama or Right Effort: You need to correct your effort. For that, you need to think in the right direction. The sixth, seventh and eight factors are closely related and inter-linked.
- Samma Satti or Righ Mindfulness: You need to acquire the state of mindfulness, which means to be aware of everything happening inside you and around you. This can be acquired by practicing the eighth factor.
- Samma Samadhi or Right Concentration: Lastly, you need to correct your focus and concentration. You must be fully concentrated on a subject to be aware of it and understand it better. Right effort, mindfulness, and concentration can only be acquired by meditation; hence, meditation is an important tool of Buddhism.

By following these eight factors, you live a balanced, composed and smooth life devoid of all sufferings.

Kamma

Kamma refers to action and the law of action. It states that every action has a reaction. If you do bad deeds- deeds pertinent to your mind, body or speech that harm you, others or both, then you will get painful results. However, by doing good deeds, you get good results. This means if we are living a life full of hardships, then it is a reflection of our bad deeds.

Rebirth

Buddha believed in rebirth. He stated that the reason why some people are born rich or poor is because of the deeds they did in their previous lives. According to him, a person is born many times and rebirth goes beyond the human realm. A person can be born as an animal, a bird, or even a spirit. The different realms that exist include human realm, grim and lower realms, ghost realm, animal and bird realm, and heavenly realm. Human begins can come or go into any of these realms.

No Creator Or God

Buddha also believed that there is no God and we are completely responsible for our own actions or kamma. If you are wealthy or poor, good or bad, evil or pure, it is entirely due to your own actions.

Illusion Of Your Soul

According to Buddha, there is no soul. Living beings are formed of their actions, activities, and parts. If you separate the body parts, the being would cease to live. This means that it is your body parts and actions that make you and not your soul. Rebirth does not require any soul too. Buddhists explain this notion beautifully with the example of lighting a candle. When a candle is about to extinguish, you take another one and light it with the help of the previous one. The previous one expires and the fresh one starts burning bright. There does exist a causal link between the two candles, but nothing went across. Similarly, there is a connection between your old and new life, but no soul goes across.

These are the fundamentals of Buddhism and precisely what you need to follow to practice Buddhism in your routine life. One more thing; you don't need to undergo any sort of religious or conversion ceremony to become a Buddhist. Most Buddhists don't even call themselves by this term. Although some Buddhists practice the ritual of accepting the '3 refuges' and consenting to keep the '5 percepts', but these services are optional. To become a Buddhist, you just need to make a decision in your heart and abide by the teachings of Buddhism.

So how can you benefit from Buddhism?

Chapter 3: How You Can Benefit From Buddhism

Buddhism can benefit you in a number of ways. First, it helps you understand that you need to be aware of the present moment and live in it instead of dwelling in the past regrets or future concerns for living a happy life.

It also helps you correct your thoughts, speech, actions and behaviors that harm you or anybody around you. Hence, Buddhism helps you become kinder, more compassionate, and generous with others. When you spread love, you get love in return because one of the prominent teachings of this philosophy is 'as you sow, so shall you reap.'

Buddhism helps you develop the right state of mind and unleash your mind's full potential for living a content and amazing life. Buddha said, *'To enjoy good health, to bring true happiness to one's family, to bring peace to all, one must first discipline and control one's own mind. If a man can control his mind, he can find the way to Enlightenment, and all wisdom and virtue will naturally come to him.'*

So when you work on correcting what goes in your mind, you are able to get rid of all sorts of negativity and pessimism and are able to think positively. The moment positive thoughts inhabit your mind, everything in your life starts straightening up. Your thoughts, feelings, emotions, and behaviors- all become right and as a result, you are able to live a comfortable life clear of all sufferings.

Therefore, Buddhism can help you achieve exactly what's missing from your life- peace and happiness.

'The mind is everything- what you think, you become.'-Buddha

Now that we have covered the basics of Buddhism, let us move on to discussing how you can practice it in your daily life.

Chapter 4: Fighting Stress, Anxiety And Depression With Buddhism

Stress, anxiety, and depression are three of the most commonly experienced mental conditions. A survey showed 80 percent Americans frequently experience stress and anxiety, 34 percent suffered from depression at least once in three months, 13 percent were diagnosed with chronic depression or anxiety disorder and 9 percent have considered suicide as the ultimate option due to their stress and depression problems. These statistics are enough to validate that these conditions are indeed extremely disturbing.

If you are experiencing or frequently go through these issues, then Buddhism offers you the perfect solution. You can easily battle all sorts of stress, anxiety and depression conditions with the help of various Buddhism practices and teachings.

Eliminate Stress And Depression With Meditation

Buddhism clearly defines that you are what you think. So if you are going to think negatively, then it is likely to cause stress, nervousness and anxiousness, which if not controlled promptly can result in depression. In addition, you found out in the previous chapter that right mindfulness and right concentration help you clarify your thoughts. Therefore, to get rid of stress and depression, you need to cleanse your thoughts, and the best way to acquire right mindfulness and concentration is via meditation.

Many scientific researches have proven that meditation helps develop and strengthen your hippocampus- a region of your brain closely associated with depression. When your hippocampus improves in size and strength, it helps you fight stress and anxiousness easily. A study by a Harvard scientist also showed that meditation helps increase the gray matter in your prefrontal cortex and people who have more gray matter in this region undergo anxiety and depression less often. This shows that science backs what Buddhism states and supports meditation.

Meditation- How to Do it

Meditating with full concentration isn't that simple, but it isn't impossible either. With practice and perseverance, you can unlock its true power and use it to your advantage. There are various kinds of meditation, but one of the commonly practiced one in Buddhism is Zazen or seated meditation.

To practice it, you need to comfortably sit on an exercise mat, or on the floor, or you can also use Zafu, which is a soft, comfortable meditation cushion. Next, you need to either cross both your legs referred to as lotus pose, or you could even extend them forward, depending on what is most comfortable for you. Make sure to choose a quiet spot to meditate and switch off all sorts of gadgets and electronics, including the television, mobile phone, and computer. Next, close your eyes to avoid getting distracted and try hearing your breath and focus completely on it. It is okay if your concentration breaks up, or you aren't even able to focus on your breath at first. This isn't a race, so you should pace yourself and take as much time as you need. Try sitting still for just five minutes. If you are a beginner, it will take you a few days to maintain your concentration for as little as five minutes, so don't give up. Once you are able to focus for five minutes, you need to start extending the duration. Ensure to focus only on your breath and body movements. By routine practice, you'll soon be able to enter a trance-like state wherein you'll be better able to analyze your thoughts and get insight into your mind. This will help you identify the poisonous and destructive thoughts harboring in your mind, so you can work on eliminating them. When your stress and anxiety inducing thoughts are discarded from your mind, your condition automatically starts improving. Make sure to make room for meditation in your daily life, even if it is for five to ten minutes. With time, you'll start noticing its benefits and you will automatically start prolonging your meditation sessions.

'We are shaped by our thoughts; we become what we think. When the mind is pure, joy follows like a shadow that never leaves.' - Buddha

Mudras For Fighting Stress

While meditating, you can also use a mudra. A mudra is a hand position. It is believed that each part of your hand produces a reflex action in a certain part of your brain, so by using those connections, you are able to produce different kinds of effects. Mudras lock and guide the energy flow as well as reflex to your brain. Hence, you can use different mudras to connect with the portions of your brain that generate neurotransmitters decreasing stress and promoting happiness. One of the most effective mudras for fighting stress and anxiety is the Tse mudra.

Using Tse Mudra

Tse mudra helps drive away all sorts of sadness, anxiety, nervousness, depression, and fear. In addition, it is believed it helps in averting bad luck and misfortune as well. It also helps enhance your mental and intuitive powers and increases your aura as it affects your body's water element.

To practice it, sit comfortably and place your hands on your thighs. Place your thumb on your little finger's root and use the fingers to cover your thumb. Begin inhaling via your nose. Keep your eyes closed. Practice it seven to nine times a day for great results.

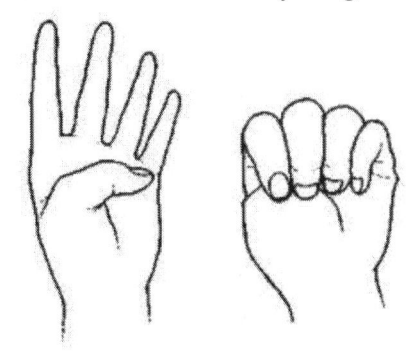

Starting Your Day With Positive Motivation And Thoughts

Buddha clearly stated that to reach the state of nirvana, you need to practice the eightfold path. You need to correct your actions, speech, livelihood, thought, effort, concentration, mindfulness, and view. When these factors are corrected, you start feeling light and peaceful inside, and will soon be cleansed of all sorts of stress and anxiousness. The first step to doing this is to infuse positive thoughts in your mind. While meditation and mudras do help you unlock your mind's power, you cannot fully unleash it until you are motivated and try making an effort.

A helpful technique that can encourage you to make a difference in your life and remove stress from it is to start your day with healthy and positive thoughts. These thoughts will help anxiety and depression disappear from your life for good. So when you wake up daily, you need to create a positive thought, ruminate on it and chant it for five minutes and use it as your motivation. You could use suggestions like:

- I attempt to release stress with every breath and make my life more peaceful.
- I am a conduit of serenity and calmness.
- My life is peaceful and I am pleased with it.
- I spread positivity everywhere I go.
- Positive energy flows through me all the time

Affirmations of this sort shape positive thinking in you and as you already know, you are what you think.

Implement these strategies and techniques from Buddhism in your life to practice the philosophy for alleviating depression and all sorts of mental imbalances from your life.

Chapter 5: Becoming Happier With Buddhism

By practicing Buddhism in your daily life, you can easily attain happiness, joy and tranquility. Let us share some Buddhism practices with you that can infuse cheerfulness and contentment in your life.

Exercise Mindfulness To Become Aware Of Your Blessings

Mindfulness refers to being cognizant of the present moment and everything it holds, including the blessings. Buddha said that people are unhappy because they live in either the past or their future and completely ignore the present. If they realized how beautiful and important the present is, they would stop worrying. To understand the significance of the present, you need to practice mindfulness. This helps you become conscious of your thoughts, helping you discern between good and bad ones, so you can nurture the happy thoughts. Plus, it helps you identify and assess the beauty involved in everything around us, which helps you realize how truly blessed you are and makes you happy.

Here are a few mindfulness-based practices that you need to practice to become truly happy.

Mindful Observation

Mindful observation helps you observe nature in a clearer manner, helping you understand its benefits. Take any natural object and start observing it. For instance, you could take a leaf and examine it in-depth. Look at its veins, its texture, and shape and feel that leaf with your hand. Look at that leaf as if you haven't seen anything like this before. This keen observation will help you understand what an amazing creation that leaf is and with constant practice, you'll be able to observe everything in the same manner. Its benefits? Well, for starters, you'll be able to identify all your blessings in an instant and be appreciative of them, which would obviously increase happiness in your life.

Mindful Appreciation

Make a list of four to five things you are thankful for every day. This helps you spot the blessings you have been showered with to be thankful to the universe for what you have. What happens when you express your gratitude to the universe? It starts throwing even better things and opportunities towards you.

To practice this, find any four or five things or people that normally go unnoticed by you and dig deeper into their origin, impact on your life and benefits. For instance, some of the important things and people that are often ignored by you include gas, electricity, your spouse, parents, table, chair, food, comfortable bed and the likes. Find out your five blessings, understand their significance, and then pay your gratitude for them to the universe. This practice will ground you into your present, appreciate it, and be more thankful for all that you have. As a result, you'll start enjoying your life more than ever.

Anjali Mudra for Happiness

When you meditate, practice Anjali mudra to become more mindful, happy and appreciative of all that you have now. To practice it, join your hands together in the 'namaste' pose and maintain this position for as long as it is convenient for you.

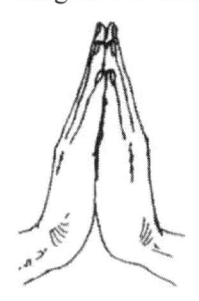

Chapter 6: Buddhism Practices For Improving Your Health And Sleep Related Problems

By applying different Buddhism practices in your routine, you can use it to improve your health, lose weight and sleep better than before. Let us find out how Buddhism can provide you with these benefits.

Offering Food To Buddha

Offering food to Buddha is one of the commonly practiced exercises by Buddhists. It is a simple act that helps you make healthy choices when it comes to eating, which improves your health and helps you lose weight easily. To practice this technique, you need to imagine that healthy food comprises of blissful, healthy nectar, which enhances your wisdom and health. Then, envision that Buddha is a beautiful light inside your heart. Whenever you eat something, you are offering that nectar to your Buddha and are consequently nourishing your heart and mind.

Visualize this peaceful thought and feel that you are actually feeding the Buddha inside you via whatever you eat. When you know you have to nourish the light inside you, you'll be motivated to eat all that is healthy and beneficial for you, removing unhealthy foods from your life. By eating healthy, you are able to stay fit. In addition, good food stabilizes your digestion and studies prove that a smooth digestion process helps you sleep easily and comfortably too.

Mindful Eating

Whenever you eat something, try to chew each bite slowly and savor its flavor and texture. Try enjoying each bite as if it's the last one ever and become more mindful of everything that you are chewing and swallowing. This act of mindful eating helps you eat slowly and when you eat slowly, you become full by eating a small amount of food, which helps you avoid eating enormous amounts of foods and reduces your chances of becoming obese. In addition, it helps you become more appreciative of the wonderful things you eat.

Mudras For Losing Weight, Improving Health, And Sleeping Better

You can also use the power of mudras to become healthier, slimmer, and sleep better.

Prithvi Mudra

Prithvi mudra helps you become mentally and physically fit. It helps you fight osteoporosis, boosts your vitality, and prevents skin dryness, hair loss, stomach ulcers, and aging. To practice it, touch your thumb and ring finger and keep the other three fingers straight. Do it for 10 minutes thrice a day to become stronger and powerful.

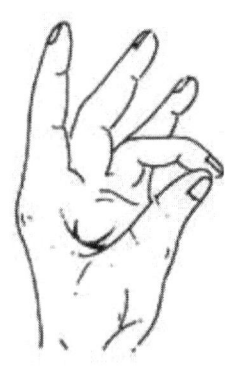

Surya Mudra

Surya mudra is excellent for losing weight, becoming energized, and relaxing your body. To exercise it, place your ring finger at your thumb's base and place your thumb over it. Straighten the other fingers. Practice it for 5 to 45 minutes daily to have an attractive body.

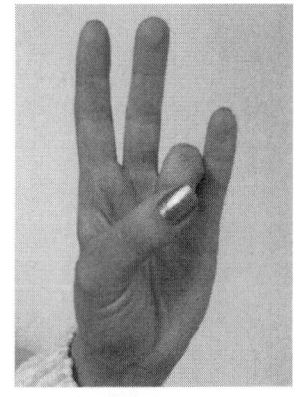

Shakti Mudra

Shakti mudra strengthens your respiratory process and muscles, helps your body fight stress, relieves your tension, and in turn helps you battle insomnia and sleep better. To practice it, touch your little and ring fingers of the right hand with those of the left one and rest your thumb in your palm. Bend the rest of your fingers and maintain this pose for 15 minutes.

Practice these strategies to become mentally and physically healthy

Chapter 7: How To Improve Your Relationships And Professional Life With Buddhism

Buddhism helps you balance your complete life, which means that by practicing it, you can incorporate harmony and betterment into every aspect of your life, including your relationships as well as professional life. Here are some Buddhism principles and practices that can help you improve your love life and other relationships as well as enjoy better career opportunities.

Practice Right Livelihood

First, you need to vow to yourself that you won't indulge in any of the five careers that Buddha prohibited you from. By doing this, you are able to get rid of all the negativity those negative careers bring in your life. Consequently, the universe offers you better career opportunities.

Secondly, you need to try opting for a career option that gives you a chance to make a positive difference in the society. Do something that benefits others. By helping others, you will infuse more positivity into your life and positivity will attract better things towards you.

Become Mindful Of Your Relationships

To improve your relationships, you need to start becoming more mindful of them. Take a paper and pen and write down all details pertinent to a relationship that you want to work on. For instance, if it's your relationship with your father that is experiencing a rocky phase, write down everything you are experiencing followed by all the times your father helped you and loved you. You need to focus on finding all the positives related to this relationship to understand its importance in your life. Moreover, while describing the bad part of the relationship, do ponder on your faults. By doing this, you'll realize your mistakes and will become conscious of them. This and your father's positives will motivate you to apologize to him and fix your severed relationship. You can do this with all the weak relationships in your life and improve them.

Additionally, you can use the 'love multiplier' mudra for improving your love life and relationships.

Love Multiplier Mudra

This mudra is inspired by the anahata chakra mudra. It helps increase your compassion towards others and brings in love in your life. To do it, join your hands together. Curl your middle and ring fingers inwards to form a heart shape and extend your index and little ringers. Curve your thumbs downwards and join them. Practice it for 15 minutes daily to fix and strengthen the stressed relationships in your life.

Without further ado, start implementing all the Buddhism strategies into your life and enjoy their amazing effects on your body, mind, and life.

Conclusion

Buddhism is an amazing way of life that can improve your quality of life. Start following this guide and all the Buddhism principles and techniques discussed in it to unlock a serene and truly amazing life.

Thank you again for taking the time to read this book!

I hope this book was able to help you to learn about Buddhism and how to incorporate it into your life.

The next step is to implement what you have learnt and enjoy living a Buddhist life.

If you have enjoyed this book, please be sure to leave a review and a comment to let us know how we are doing so we can continue to bring you quality ebooks.

Thank you and good luck!

Check out another book by Elias Axmar

This book is a guide that is intended to help you achieve a mindful and stress-free life through the concepts of mindfulness meditation.

Here, mindfulness meditation will be thoroughly discussed. It addresses the fact that there are a handful of reasons why you should appreciate the benefits of mindfulness. While others want a defense against the overload of trivial matters, some aim to be mindful for a sense of inner peace. Some just wish to relax and take a break from most of their worries. With all the people you talk to, the obligations that need attention, and all the other demands of everyday life, the knowledge on mindfulness can be beneficial.

THE MINDFULNESS MEDITATION GUIDE FOR A MINDFUL AND STRESS-FREE LIFE

ELIAS AXMAR

Printed in Great Britain
by Amazon